W9-CNU-911

GRAND LEDGE PUBLIC SCHOOLS
Greenwood Library

TALKABOUT

Light

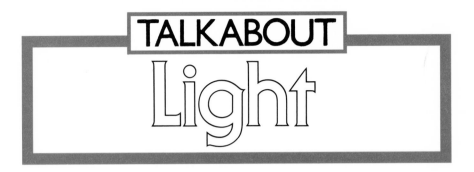

TALKABOUT
Light

Text: Angela Webb
Photography: Chris Fairclough

GRAND LEDGE PUBLIC SCHOOLS
Greenwood Library

Franklin Watts
London/New York/Sydney/Toronto

© 1988 Franklin Watts

First published in Great Britain by

Franklin Watts
12a Golden Square
London W1

First published in the USA by

Franklin Watts Inc
387 Park Avenue South
New York 10016

ISBN: UK edition 0 86313 551 X

ISBN: US edition 0–531–10455–9
Library of Congress
Catalog Card No: 87–50586

Consultant: Henry Pluckrose
Editor: Ruth Thomson
Design: Edward Kinsey
Additional photographs: Zefa

Typesetting: Keyspools Ltd
Printed in Hong Kong

About this book

This book has been written for young children – in the playgroup, school and at home.

Its aim is to increase children's awareness of the world around them and to promote thought and discussion about topics of scientific interest.

The book draws on examples from a child's own environment. The activities and experiments suggested are simple enough for children to conduct themselves, with only a little help from an adult, using objects and materials which will be familiar to them.

Children will gain most from the book if the book is used together with practical activities. Such experiences will help to consolidate knowledge and also suggest new ideas for further exploration and experimentation.

The themes explored in this book include:

Light enables us to see.
Daylight comes from the sun.
Light also comes from several other sources.
Light travels in straight lines.
Light is used by plants.

Just imagine what it would be like
if it were dark all the time.

Could you see to run
and play . . .

or draw pictures?

GRAND LEDGE PUBLIC SCHOOLS
Greenwood Library

Could you find your way
around a room
if you were wearing
a blindfold?

When is it dark?
Why isn't it dark during the day?
Where does light come from?

Light comes from the sun.
The day begins
when the sun rises in the morning . . .

and ends
when the sun sets
in the evening.

Sunlight is very bright.
Never look straight into the sun.
It can damage your eyes.

Even when clouds hide the sun,
there is enough sunlight
for us to see by.

At night, the moon reflects sunlight to the earth.

Where else does light come from?
Faint light comes from stars.

People cannot see very well when it is dark.
Some animals can see much better than people at night.

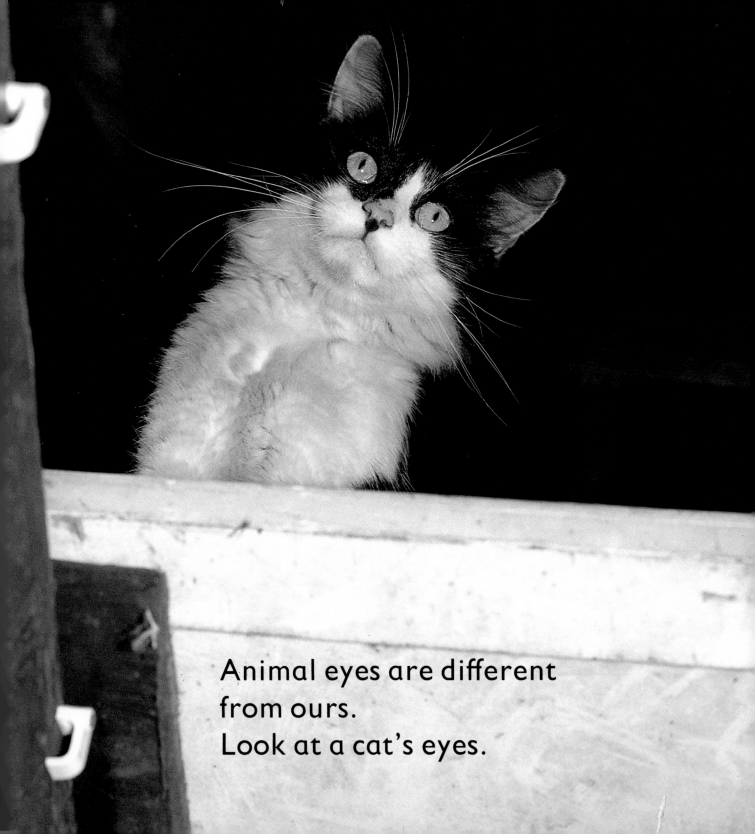

Animal eyes are different
from ours.
Look at a cat's eyes.

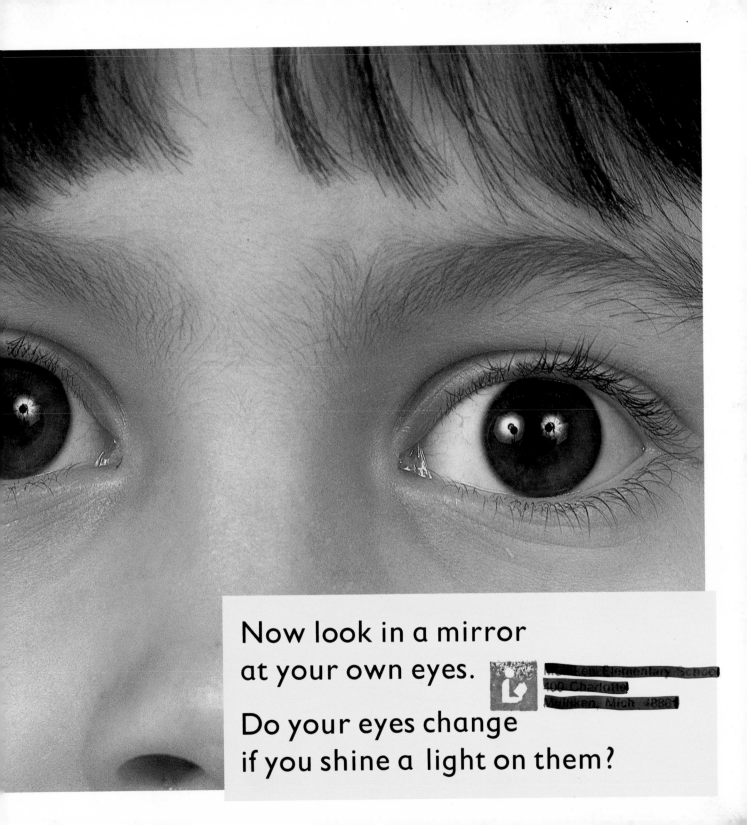

Now look in a mirror
at your own eyes.

Do your eyes change
if you shine a light on them?

Where else do we see light?

Fire gives out light.

People used to burn candles
to get light.

Now we use electric lights . . .

and flashlights
powered by batteries.

How does light shine?
Does it go in a straight line?

Cut a hole in the middle
of both ends of a shoebox.

Shine a light through one hole.
Does light come out of the other?

Shine a light into a funnel. What happens to the beam?

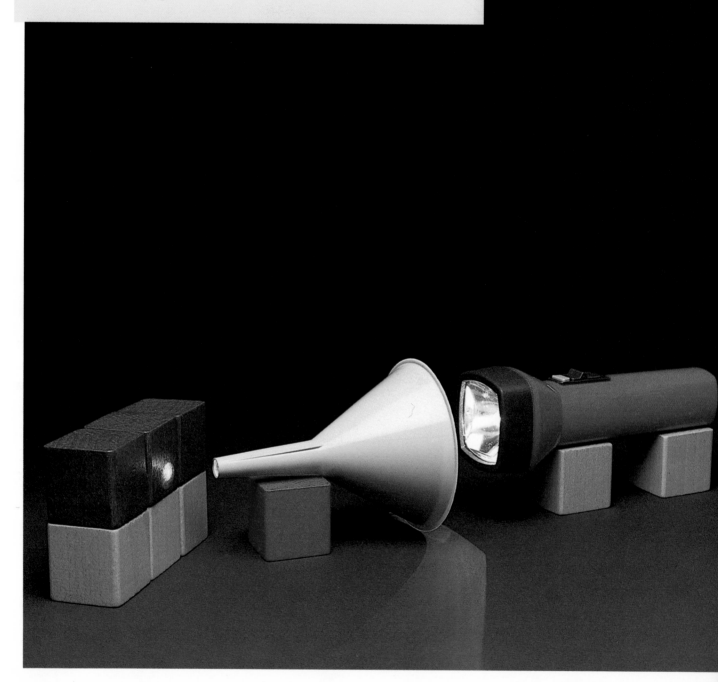

These plants need light to grow.
Light turns the leaves green.

Leave a brick on the grass
for a week.
What do you notice
when you take the brick away?

Put some cress seeds
on two separate dishes.
Water them.

Leave one dish in the light
and cover the other one.
What happens?

Light allows us to see things.
It helps make our world
more beautiful!